WESTCOUNTRY C

Meat

compiled and edited by
Fiona James

Supported by Objective 5b
EAGGF Funds

Supported by Food From
Britain and DEFRA

DEFRA
Department for
Environment,
Food & Rural Affairs

West Country Meat

From the smallest household to the largest hotel or restaurant the West Country cook or chef has access to the best meat in the world! The grazing pastures, heather clad uplands and salt marshes of the South West are famed for producing meat of the highest quality. Furthermore our butchers are renowned for giving "Value for Money" and long may the traditional family butchers' businesses survive.

The foundations of our meat industry lie in the native breeds, the South Devon and Devon Red Ruby Beef Cattle; at least eleven South West sheep breeds such as the Exmoor Horn; and traditional pigs such as the Gloucester Old Spot. These longstanding natives of the West Country give character and quality to our meat and are well supplemented by excellent game and poultry.

Good meat is all about breed, feed, welfare, friendly slaughter, hanging, butchery and cooking. Here in the South West we have all the quality inputs to provide roasts, pies, casseroles, grills and a multitude of variations, resulting in meat cookery second to none.

Albert Beer
1st May 2002

CONTENTS

LAMB AND BEEF ... 3
Roast Chump of Lamb, Shallots, Cherry Tomatoes and Thyme with Wild Garlic Mash ... 7
Charcoal Grilled Brochette of Lamb with Herbs ... 9
Loin of Lamb in Filo with Vine Leaves served with a Lemon Mint Sauce ... 10
Pan Roasted Breast of Lamb with Saffron, Tomato, and Garlic Bread ... 11
Leg of Cotswold Lamb baked in Hay with Herb Butter ... 13
Cornish Lamb Confit with Caper Sauce ... 15
Best end of Lamb with Port and Rosemary Sauce ... 17
Butterflied Leg of Lamb baked in a Salt Paste Crust ... 18
Devilled Steaks ... 19
Marinated Steaks ... 21
Cornish Beef Carpaccio ... 23
Christmas Spiced Beef ... 24
Noodle Salad with Chilli Beef Cups ... 25
Pan Fried Fillet of Devon Beef on Roasted Vegetables with Roasted Cherry Tomato Dressing ... 27

PORK, BACON AND SAUSAGES ... 29
Denhay Air Dried Ham with Asparagus ... 31
Grilled Capricorn Goats Cheese with Crispy Bacon Salad ... 32
Roast Pork with Bacon and Spinach Stuffing ... 33
Denhay Cheddar and Bacon Pudding ... 35
Pork Fillet with Apricots and West Country Cider ... 36
Devon Pork in Mustard Sauce ... 37
Pilgrims Pork Fillet with Bacon and Sage ... 39
Farmers' Market Sausage Casserole ... 41

CHICKEN AND DUCK ... 43
Darts Farm Spicy Chicken Salad ... 45
Chicken Parcels with Devon Blue Sauce ... 47
Simple Creamy Chicken Pie ... 49
Black Pepper and Lemon Chicken ... 50
Roast Duck Breasts with Raspberries and Balsamic Vinegar ... 51
Duck Breast with Orange and Cointreau Sauce ... 53
Duck Breast with Victoria Plum Sauce and Chive Rosti ... 54
Roast Duck with Plum and Mustard Sauce ... 55

GAME AND VENISON ... 57
Red Ruby Beef and Game Casserole ... 58
Venison Minute Steaks in Mushroom Sauce ... 59
Venison Liver with a Wild Mushroom, Smoked Bacon & Juniper Berry Sauce ... 60
Roast Loin of Venison with Black Pudding and a Black Treacle Sauce ... 61

Acknowledgements ... 62
Index ... 63

Lamb & Beef

ROAST CHUMP OF LAMB, SHALLOTS, CHERRY TOMATOES AND THYME WITH WILD GARLIC MASH

Red Snapper
1 Chandos Road
Redland
Bristol
0117 973 7999

Westcountry Cooking Award Winner:
Best Restaurant in Somerset 2001
Red Snapper is a highly rated fish restaurant near the centre of Bristol. Chef/owner John Raines is dedicated to using top quality food in season when flavours are at their peak, ensuring that the menu evolves continually.

Marinade the lamb in pomace oil, chopped garlic and a few sprigs of thyme for 1 to 5 days.

For the Sauce:

Reduce the stock, wine and redcurrant jelly with some thyme by about half. Season to taste.

Peel and boil the potatoes and mash with 75g (3oz) of the butter and the chopped, blanched wild garlic.

Roast the shallots in the hot oven in a dish with 25g (1 oz) of butter and a little brown sugar until they caramelise and are soft, (20 – 30 minutes) and set aside.

Heat a heavy ovenproof pan. Season the lamb and seal all sides until well coloured. Place in the oven for 15-20 minutes.

Remove from the oven and rest for 10 minutes.

Meanwhile reheat the shallots in the sauce, add half of the cherry tomatoes a minute before serving.

Place a generous spoonful of the mash into the centre of each warmed plate. Arrange the shallots, cherry tomatoes and sauce around the mash. Carve the lamb into 5 mm (¼ inch) slices and arrange on top of the mash.

Garnish with a sprig of thyme or wild garlic.

Photo: Sam Bailey

Main Course
Serves 4

Preparation Time:
30 mins

Cooking Time:
1 hour

Oven Temperature:
200°C; 400°F; Gas Mark 6

Marinade Time:
up to 5 days

Ingredients:
- 4 x 175g – 225g (6-8oz) ready trimmed lamb chumps (1mm of fat left on)
- 4 medium potatoes for mash
- 1 handful of wild garlic blanched
- 110g (4oz) butter
- 1 punnet cherry tomatoes
- 20 shallots peeled with root intact
- 1 tbsp brown sugar
- bunch thyme
- ½ litre (¾ pint) good chicken stock
- 50g (2oz) redcurrant jelly
- ½ bottle red wine
- 4 cloves garlic
- 150 ml (5 floz) pomace oil

CHARCOAL GRILLED BROCHETTE OF LAMB WITH HERBS

The Agaric
Ashburton
01364 654478

The menu at the Agaric constantly evolves, combining traditional and contemporary cuisine. They always use local, seasonal produce from small suppliers who grow varieties of salad, fruit and vegetables. Nick Coiley is the chef at the Agaric, and the restaurant is stylish but relaxed, focussing on comfort and the quality of the eating experience.

Mix the herbs, orange zest and olive oil with the diced lamb. Make up onto metal skewers with a piece of bay leaf in between. Leave to marinade for up to three hours.

While the potatoes are still warm mix with the dressing and transfer to a pottery serving dish.

Charcoal grill or cook under the grill for 5-10 minutes depending on how you like your lamb.

Serve with the potato and a green salad.

Main Course
Serves 4

Preparation Time:
25 mins

Cooking Time:
15 mins

Marinade Time:
3 hours

Served with a potato herb salad
Ingredients:
- 800g (1lb 10oz) of diced and trimmed leg of lamb (cut into 2.5 cm/1 inch cubes)
- bay leaves, thyme, rosemary, parsley, chopped roughly, a handful of each
- olive oil
- zest of one orange

Herb Potato Salad:
- 1kg (2lb) small new potatoes, cooked until just tender and cut into large dice
- whizz the following in a blender:
- large bunch of mint
- rosemary, bronze fennel, dill
- 1 large clove of garlic, peeled and chopped
- 1 tbsp vinegar
- 4 tbsp virgin olive oil
- rock salt

LOIN OF LAMB IN FILO WITH VINE LEAVES SERVED WITH A LEMON MINT SAUCE

Main Course
Serves 4

Preparation Time:
30 mins

Cooking Time:
10 mins

Oven Temperature:
Gas Mark 7; 425°F; 220°C

Ingredients:
- 2 best ends of lamb chined
- 12 vine leaves either fresh, blanched or packet
- 4 sheets filo pastry
- 50g (2 oz) melted butter
- salt and pepper

Sauce:
- grated lemon rind and juice ½ lemon
- 150 ml (5floz) strong lamb stock
- 1 tbsp chopped fresh mint
- 1 chopped shallot, reduced with (50ml) white wine
- 2 egg yolks

Joyce Molyneux

Joyce formerly ran the famous Carved Angel in Dartmouth but has now retired and lives in Bath.

Take the chine bone off the lamb, remove the fillets and trim to remove silver skin.

Cut each in half to give two portions. Make stock with the bone and meat trimmings, reduce and cool.

Wrap each piece of lamb in 3 vine leaves and season.

To wrap: brush a sheet of filo pastry with melted butter and cut in half, and place one half on top of the other so that it is double thickness. Put meat on one end of filo, fold in the sides and roll up to make a parcel. Repeat for the other three pieces of meat.

Put on a baking tray and brush with the remaining butter. Cook in a hot oven for 10 minutes and allow to rest in a warm place for a further 5 minutes. This gives a pink finish to the lamb, cook an extra 5 minutes if you prefer it well done. Cut each in half and serve on a little of the sauce.

Sauce:

Put the shallot and wine in a pan and reduce until almost dry. Tip into a blender, add lemon rind and juice, seasoning and egg yolks. Bring the stock to a rolling boil and set the blender going. Pour in the stock to the moving blender. Blend well, return to pan add mint and check the seasoning.

Accompanying vegetables: new potatoes and summer vegetables such broad beans or runner beans.

PAN ROASTED BREAST OF LAMB WITH SAFFRON, TOMATO, AND GARLIC BREAD

The Galley
Topsham
Exeter
01392 876078
www.galleyrestaurant.co.uk
Chef: Paul da Costa Greaves

Winner of Westcountry Cooking Award: Best Restaurant in Devon 2001 and 2002 and Best Restaurant in the South West Region 2002. Primarily fish and shellfish specialists reflecting a contemporary style of exotic, healthy and elegant food freshly prepared using the finest West Country ingredients. The Galley has just been awarded 2 AA Rosettes and 4 Diamonds for their accommodation.

The breast of lamb is a cut of meat taken from the belly, it is full of flavour and very affordable. Make sure it has been skinned, boned and any excess fat removed. One breast should be enough for 2 portions. Once cut into 2, roll the lamb lengthways and tie tightly.

Put the saffron threads and chardonnay in a saucepan and gently heat to bloom and soften the saffron. Remove from the heat and allow to cool. Whisk in the olive oil and vegetable oil and season to taste with salt and pepper to form a vinaigrette.

Place the lamb in a large pan. Add the vinaigrette, white wine vinegar, tomato juice, shallots, rosemary and garlic. Cover the pot with a lid and place on a high heat to seal in the flavours.

Reduce the heat and simmer until tender for approx. 90 to 120 mins. 15 minutes prior to serving add the cherry tomatoes, lime zest, parsley and coriander leaves.

Serve with the garlic bread slices and a green salad.

Main Course
Serves 4

Preparation Time:
30 mins

Cooking Time:
90-120 mins

Ingredients:
- 1 pinch saffron
- 125 ml (4 floz) chardonnay
- 25 ml (¾ floz) white wine vinegar
- 75 ml (2 ½ floz) extra virgin olive oil
- 75 ml (2 ½ floz) vegetable oil
- 100 ml (3 floz) tomato juice
- sea salt
- ground black pepper
- 4 portions of lamb breast rolled and tied
- 150g (5oz) cherry tomatoes cut in half or 50g (2oz) sun dried tomatoes coarsely chopped
- 3 shallots thinly sliced
- 1 tbsp crushed garlic
- zest of a lime
- 15g / 1 tbsp roughly chopped flat leaf parsley
- 15g / 1 tbsp roughly chopped coriander leaves
- 1 sprig of rosemary
- crusty bread, sliced, toasted and rubbed with raw garlic.

LEG OF COTSWOLD LAMB BAKED IN HAY WITH HERB BUTTER

Windrush House
Hazelton
Cheltenham
01451 860364

Winner of Westcountry Cooking Award: Best Farmhouse Food in Gloucestershire 2001
1 mile from the A40, the house is in the unspoilt village of Hazelton near the medieval church. Guests enjoy home baked bread and home made soups together with traditional dishes and fresh vegetables.

Wipe the leg dry with a kitchen cloth and then coat liberally with the butter, and season with the sea salt and black pepper.

Take 2 large pieces of tin foil and lay them criss-cross across the base of a roasting tin.

On the base of the roasting tin lay some hay and place the lamb on top of it, sprinkle with chopped herbs and cover with hay.

Wrap the whole tray tightly with the tin foil so that the hay does not catch fire and bake at 375°F 190°C or Gas Mark 5 for 3 hours. Do not open the parcel to baste or look at the meat.

Serve with roast potatoes, parsnips and seasonal vegetables.

Preparation Time:
15 mins

Cooking Time:
3 hours

Oven Temperature:
Gas Mark 5; 375°F; 190°C

Ingredients:
- 3 kg (6 – 7 lb) leg of lamb
- 110g (4 oz) softened butter
- chopped herbs such as parsley, coriander, lemon thyme or rosemary
- sea salt
- freshly ground black pepper
- clean meadow hay

CORNISH LAMB CONFIT WITH CAPER SAUCE

The Pencubbit Hotel
Lamellion Cross, Liskeard
Cornwall
01579 342694

2001 Winner of Westcountry Cooking Award:
Best Hotel in Cornwall
Best Hotel in South West

Quality independent hotel situated just outside the historic market town of Liskeard. Emphasis is placed on the cuisine at Pencubitt with the very best ingredients being sourced locally to produce the highest quality dishes, absolutely fresh and full of flavour.

Blend marinade ingredients together into a paste in the blender.
Rub the paste on to the lamb and leave to marinade for between 24 – 48 hours in the fridge.
Scrape off the marinade paste, roll the meat tightly and tie with string.
Wrap tightly in a couple of layers of tin foil and place on baking tray.
Cook in a slow oven for 4.5 to 5 hours.
Leave to cool, and when cool enough to handle remove the foil, saving any juices and wrap tightly in cling film to give an even shape. Refrigerate for at least 24 hours.

To make the sauce:
Reduce the white wine until syrupy. Add the lamb stock and the saved meat juices, and reduce until it has a nice syrupy consistency.
Thicken with double cream and flavour with capers or any fresh herbs.

To serve:
Cut the lamb into thick slices (2-3cm) and slowly reheat in the well reduced lamb stock sauce.
Serve with the sauce and some fresh vegetables.
It may take a while – but is the most delicious lamb dish you'll ever try!

Suggested serving accompaniments: fondant potato, buttered spinach, fine green beans, swede.

Main Course
Serves 4

Preparation Time:
1 hour

Cooking Time:
4.5 – 5 hours

Marinade Time:
24-48 hours
+ 24 hours Refrigeration time

Oven Temperature:
Gas Mark 1; 275°F; 140°C

Ingredients:
- 1 boned shoulder (3 kg or 6-7lb) Cornish lamb
- 1.2 litres (2 pints) lamb stock (made from the bones of the shoulder)
- 150ml (5floz) white wine
- 2 tbsp double cream
- 1 dspn capers

Marinade:
- 50g (2oz) sea salt
- 20g (¾ oz) soft brown sugar
- 1 onion
- 1 head garlic
- bunch of thyme, rosemary, mint
- 2 bay leaves
- zest of one lemon

LAMB AND BEEF

BEST END OF LAMB WITH PORT AND ROSEMARY SAUCE

Jacqueline's Restaurant and Tea Rooms
Warminster
Wilts
01985 217373

Regional Winner of Westcountry Cooking Award for Best Café /Tearoom in the South West 2001

Jacqueline's offers high quality food served in a relaxed atmosphere with old fashioned courtesy. Wherever possible local produce is featured and the menu frequently altered to take full advantage of the seasonal wealth of West Country ingredients.

Pre heat the oven to Gas Mark 7, 425°F/220°C. Put the reserved fat from the lamb into a heavy frying pan and gently heat it until it starts to render down, just enough to lightly oil the pan. Remove the lumps of fat and then sear the lamb joints on all sides until nicely caramelised.

Place in a baking tray, bone side up and roast in the top of the pre heated oven. For rare lamb this takes 8-9 minutes. Increase the time for well done lamb, remove from the oven and allow to rest for 10 minutes.

Whilst the lamb is resting prepare the sauce, drain most of the juices from the pan and add the port, redcurrant jelly and the rosemary (to impart more flavour distress the rosemary by hitting it with a rolling pin, add the twigs as well). Season with salt and freshly ground pepper and reduce to a coating consistency. If it becomes too thick it can be thinned with a little hot water. Adjust the seasoning to taste.

To serve:
Carve the meat between the bones and arrange the slices on top of the sauce and drizzle a little over them.

Suggested vegetables: parsnips, roasted, chipped or made into a rosti, orange glazed carrots.

Photo: David Wiltshire of David Wiltshire Photographers.

Main Course
Serves 4

Preparation Time:
10 mins

Cooking Time:
9-15 mins

Oven Temperature:
Gas Mark 7; 425°F; 220°C

Ingredients:
- 2 x best end lamb cut in half. This give four ribs per portion. Ask your butcher to French trim and chine them and to reserve some of the discarded fat – around 50-75g (2-3oz)
- 400ml (14 floz) ruby port
- 200g (7oz) redcurrant jelly
- 2 or 3 sprigs of rosemary
- salt and freshly ground black pepper

BUTTERFLIED LEG OF LAMB BAKED IN A SALT PASTE CRUST

Main Course
Serves 4

Preparation Time: 30 mins

Cooking Time: 1 ½ hours

Marinade Time: 2-24 hours

Oven Temperature:
Gas Mark 7; 425°F; 220°C

Ingredients:
1 x 1.5kg (3 ½ lb) leg of lamb*

For the marinade:
- 1 medium onion*
- 2 tbsp oyster, plum or soy sauce
- 2.5cm (1 inch) ginger*
- 2 tbsp redcurrant jelly
- 100ml (3 floz) red wine
- rosemary* (1 tbsp)
- 2 tbsp olive oil

For the salt paste crust:
- 250g (9oz) coarse salt
- 250g (9oz) plain flour
- about 175ml (6 floz) cold water
- rosemary* (minimum 2 tbsp)
- freshly ground black pepper

*Mise en place:
- bone the leg of lamb
- re-weigh
- finely chop the onion
- grate the ginger
- finely chop the herbs

©Caroline Yates, Confident Cooking,
PO Box 841, Devizes SN10 4UX
01380 812846

Under the name Confident Cooking, Caroline Yates runs cookery demonstrations, practical day workshops and weekend residential courses from her own semi professional kitchen in a renovated manor farmhouse in Wiltshire. Caroline believes passionately in food with taste and this is best sourced from local West Country producers and growers. Learn what to look for when buying the best and freshest ingredients, how to cook them simply and present them beautifully.

In a large plastic bag, mix together the marinade ingredients. Put in the lamb, tie the bag around the neck and then massage the lamb in the marinade, and turn as often as is practicable. Refrigerate overnight, or, if time is short, for at least two hours.

Pre heat the oven to Gas Mark 7, 425°F, 220°C.

To make the salt crust: mix the crust ingredients together to form a firm paste. Roll out into a rectangular sheet about ½cm (¼ inch) thick.

Remove the lamb from the marinade; strain the marinade, reserving both solids and juices, and pat the lamb dry with kitchen paper. Lay it on the salt crust, spread over the marinade solids and season with freshly ground black pepper.

Brush the edges of the salt crust with water and wrap the lamb, sealing the edges well. Transfer to a lightly oiled roasting pan and bake immediately on the middle shelf of the oven for about 45 - 50 minutes (if you have a meat thermometer, it should read 60°C) or until the crust is very brown. Remove from the oven and allow to rest in a warm place for a minimum of 30 minutes.

Heat the marinade juices and season, adding more rosemary if needed. Boil until syrupy, and pour into a sauce boat and keep warm until ready to use.

To serve: carefully remove the crust and scrape off any paste stuck to the joint. Transfer the lamb to a warm serving dish and carve with ease.

DEVILLED STEAKS

Coombe Estate
Beech Walk
Gittisham
Honiton
Devon EX14 3AB
(01404) 45576
Email: combe.estate@lineone.net
Richard Marker

The Coombe Estate is situated 2 miles west of Honiton and is home to the Gittisham Herd of Devon Ruby Reds. This particular breed is slow growing and old fashioned and are left to grow and mature at a natural pace. Growth promoters, routine antibiotics and artificial additives are not used in the production of the beef. A proper taste and texture are part of the qualities of beef and Devon "Ruby Red" beef has outstanding flavour and tenderness which shows in its marbling.

The beef is currently sold at Ottery St Mary Farmers' Market and at Mole Valley Farmers in Cullompton as well as the local shop in Gittisham.

The beef comes in the usual cuts, from fillets, sirloin and rump steaks to joints, mince and sausages. Visit Coombe Estate and see for yourselves or telephone to ask for details of their mail order service.

Ottery St Mary Farmers' Market is held on 1st Friday of each month in Hind Street car park.

This recipe is an adaption of a recipe from Tom Bridge's Recipe book, "Bridge on British Beef"

Main Course
Serves 8

Preparation Time:
15 mins

Cooking Time:
5 – 15 mins

Marinade Time:
4 hours

Ingredients:

For the Marinade:
- 45 g (3 tbsp) french mustard
- 2 cloves garlic, peeled, crushed and blended with a little oil
- 5 g (1 tsp) paprika
- 60 g (4 tbsp) demerara sugar
- 10 ml (2 tsp) dry vermouth
- pinch of fresh rosemary leaves, crushed

- 8 x 175 – 200 g (6 – 7 oz) rump steaks

Mix together the marinade in a glass bowl. Place the steaks in a bowl and pour over the marinade.

Marinate in the refrigerator for four hours.

Grill or barbecue for at least 5 minutes on each side, basting with the marinade.

MARINATED STEAKS

Beech Hayes Farm
Churchinford, Taunton
01823 601565
Beechayes@aol.com

Ruth and Nick Strange

Beech Hayes Farm produces "Happy" meat in the traditional way, within the Blackdown Hills Environmentally Sensitive Area. They carry out extensive farming with no pesticides and limited use of fertilisers.

Beech Hayes superb meat can be bought at the following farmers' markets:

Honiton – 3rd Thursday of each month
Lace Walk Car Park

Taunton – 4th Thursday of each month
High Street

Bridgwater – 2nd Friday of each month
Town Centre

Or from the farm by arrangement

Mix together the ingredients for the marinade and place the steaks in a bowl with the marinade. Cover and leave for a minimum of 6 hours, turning once.

Just before cooking, remove the steaks from the marinade and pat dry. Brush with a little olive oil and grill or fry as usual.

Boil the marinade rapidly until reduced by a half and use this to baste the cooking steaks.

Main Course:
Serves 4

Preparation Time:
15 mins

Cooking Time:
5 –15 mins

Marinade Time:
6 – 24 hours

Ingredients:
- 4 x 250 g (8 oz) steaks (sirloin or rump)

For the marinade:
- 6 crushed black peppercorns
- 25 g (1 ½ tbsp) soft brown sugar
- 5 cloves
- 10 g (2 tsp) dijon mustard
- 250 ml (8 floz) Guinness
- 5 cm (2 inches) cinnamon stick, crumbled

CORNISH BEEF CARPACCIO

The Pencubbit Hotel
Lamellion Cross
Liskeard
Cornwall
01579 342694
2001 Winner of Westcountry Cooking Awards
Best Hotel in Cornwall
Best Hotel in South West

Quality independent hotel situated just outside the historic market town of Liskeard. Emphasis is placed on the cuisine at Pencubitt with the very best ingredients being sourced locally to produce the highest quality dishes, absolutely fresh and full of flavour.

Mix together all the marinade ingredients.

Roll the beef in the marinade, cover the dish and refrigerate for 24 hours. Turn the beef three or four times during this time.

Remove the beef from the marinade and wrap in cling film.

Press the marinade through a sieve to give the dressing.

To Serve:
Slice the beef extremely thinly and allow 4/5 slices per person.

Serve with fresh rocket leaves, mature cheddar shavings and a few fresh basil leaves.

Dress the leaves and the meat with 2-3 tspns of the dressing. Add a twist of black pepper.

Starter
Serves 4

Preparation Time:
20 mins

Cooking Time:
None

Marinade Time:
24 hours

Ingredients:
- 375g (12oz) tail end of Cornish Beef fillet, trimmed of any fat

For the Marinade:
- 110ml (4floz) Balsamic vinegar
- 3 tbsp soy sauce
- 3 tbsp Worcestershire sauce
- 1 tspn crushed black peppercorns
- 225ml (8floz) red wine
- 3 chopped garlic cloves
- 450ml (16 floz) olive oil
- handful of fresh thyme, rosemary
- salt

To Serve:
- fresh basil
- good quality West Country extra mature cheddar (Quickes Cheese Ltd)
- rocket
- black pepper

CHRISTMAS SPICED BEEF

Main Course
Serves 12 or more

Preparation Time:
13 days

Cooking Time:
5 hours

Oven Temperature:
Gas mark 1; 140°C; 275°F

Ingredients:
- 2.5 – 3 kg (5 – 6 lbs) silverside or topside
- 75 g (3oz) dark muscavado sugar
- 2 cloves
- 25 g (2 tbsp) black peppercorns
- 25 g (2 tbsp) juniper berries
- 15 g (1 tbsp) allspice berries
- 2 cinnamon sticks
- sea salt
- 10 g (2 tsp) dried thyme
- 10 g (2 tsp) saltpetre (optional)
- 200 ml (7 oz) cider or water

Wild Beef
Lizzie and Richard Vines
Hillhead Farm, Chagford TQ13 8DY
01647 433433

Day One:

Place the beef into a very clean casserole dish. Massage into the joint with your fingertips adding the muscavado sugar. Cover and put in a cold larder.

Day Three – Day Eleven:

Reduce to a coarse powder the cloves, peppercorns, juniper berries, allspice, cinnamon and salt.

Stir in the thyme and saltpetre (if using).

Rub this mixture into the beef. Cover again and let the joint cure in the cold larder for nine more days, just turning the meat and rubbing the gradually liquefying spice mixture into it each day.

Day Twelve:

When the cure is completed, quickly rinse the meat under a cold tap. On no account soak it and wipe off any remaining spices with a damp cloth.

Put the joint into a heavy oval casserole to hold it snugly. Pour on the cider or water and seal the lid tightly. Place a sheet of greaseproof paper or tin foil between the pot and the lid to create a tighter seal.

Cook at 140°C 275°F Gas Mark 1 for 4 ½ to 5 hours. Do not open the pot while the meat cooks.

Let the beef rest in the unopened pot for 2 ½ to 3 hours. Then lift out the meat, letting all the juices drip back into the pot (to use in stocks or soups).

Pat the joint dry with kitchen towel, wrap it in greaseproof paper and sandwich between two boards.

Place weights of about 2 kg (4 lbs) on top and leave it in a cold larder overnight.

Day Thirteen:

Wrap the spiced beef in fresh greaseproof paper, overwrap it in foil and put it into the fridge.

Bring it back to room temperature at least 2 hours before it is to be eaten and carve into very thin slices for serving.

NOODLE SALAD WITH CHILLI BEEF CUPS

Wild Beef
Lizzie and Richard Vines
Hillhead Farm, Chagford TQ13 8DY
01647 433433

Main Course
Serves 4

Preparation Time: 30 mins

Cooking Time: 10 mins

Ingredients:
- 225g (8oz) stir-fry beef strips, wafer thin
- 200 g (7oz) thin dried egg noodles
- 40 ml (2 ½ tbsp) peanut oil
- 1 little gem lettuce
- 4 small shallots, peeled and sliced
- 3 cloves garlic, peeled and chopped
- 2 fresh chillies, seeded and cut into long strips
- 1 tbsp light soy sauce
- 1 tbsp fish sauce
- 10 g (2 tsp) sugar
- juice of 1 lime
- 50 g (2 oz) crushed roasted peanuts
- 2 spring onions, white part only thinly sliced
- 6 sprigs of coriander leaves
- 4 sprigs mint, chopped
- 2 tbsp dark soy sauce or to taste

If the strips are not pre sliced, put them in the freezer for 15 minutes to firm up, then slice as thinly as possible.

Bring to the boil a large pan of water. Add the noodles and return the water to the boil and cook until al dente. Rinse under cold water, drain and toss in 2 tsp of peanut oil.

Place the noodles on a large serving platter.

Take the little gem lettuce and separate into individual cup-shaped leaves. Reserve the largest leaves; shred the smaller ones and arrange the shredded lettuce in a ring around the noodles.

Heat the remaining 2 tbsp of oil to smoking point in a wok. Add the shallots, garlic and chillies and stir fry for around 30 seconds.

Add the beef strips and stir once.

Pour in the soy sauce and fish sauce, and toss for just 1 ½ minutes.

When the meat no longer looks raw add the sugar.

Transfer the wok contents to a bowl. When the beef morsels are cool, put them in the lettuce leaf cups, pour over the juices from the bowl, and sprinkle with the lime juice, peanuts, spring onions, coriander leaves, mint and dark soy sauce.

Place the lettuce cups on top of the noodles and serve.

PAN FRIED FILLET OF DEVON BEEF ON ROASTED VEGETABLES WITH ROASTED CHERRY TOMATO DRESSING

Browns
80 West Street
Tavistock
01822 618686

A newly opened stylish townhouse hotel and restaurant, situated in ancient Tavistock on the edge of Dartmoor. The restaurant has quickly established a reputation for imaginative and lively menus, prepared using the finest freshest ingredients.
Head Chef: Charles Hilton

Place the cherry tomatoes on a roasting tray with a little sea salt and roast in the oven Gas Mark 5 for about 8 /10 minutes. Mix the olive oil, Balsamic vinegar, mustard, garlic and parsley in a bowl, season to taste. Add the cherry tomatoes, once cooked, and keep this dressing in a warm place.

Place the diced vegetables in a roasting pan with a little olive oil and pepper and roast until tender, keep warm.

Season each beef fillet and seal in a hot frying pan, then place in a hot oven until cooked to med-rare – approximately 10 –15 minutes. Remove from the oven and allow to rest in a warm place for 5–10 minutes

To assemble the dish place a quarter of the roasted vegetables onto each plate with a fillet of beef. Finish the dish by spooning the warm tomato dressing around the fillet and garnish with a sprig of fresh chervil.

Main Course
Serves 4

Preparation Time:
30 mins

Cooking Time:
30 mins

Oven Temperature:
Gas Mark 5; 375°F; 190°C

Ingredients:
- 4 x 150g (5oz) fillet of Devon beef
- 250g (9oz) swede diced
- 250g (9oz) carrot diced
- 250g (9oz) courgette diced
- 250g (9oz) red pepper diced
- salt and pepper
- 1 punnet of cherry tomatoes
- 200ml (7floz) olive oil
- 50ml (2floz) good Balsamic vinegar
- 2 cloves garlic crushed
- ½ tsp English mustard
- 1 tbsp rough chopped flat leaf parsley
- fresh chervil

Pork, Bacon & Sausages

DENHAY AIR DRIED HAM WITH ASPARAGUS

Denhay Farms Ltd
Broadoak
Bridport
Dorset DT6 5NP
01308 422770
www.denhay.co.uk
George and Amanda Streatfeild

Denhay Farms Ltd produce superb award winning Air Dried Ham and Dry Cured Bacon, together with their Farmhouse Cheddar using the traditional skills and techniques employed in the Marshwood Vale and West Country for generations. Denhay Farm is set in an area of outstanding natural beauty and uses the original West Country cycle; lush grass to feed the dairy herd to make cheese; the whey from the cheese to feed the pigs; the muck from the pigs to fertilise the grass to feed the cows.

Denhay Air Dried Ham is known as "English prosciutto" with its own unique character.
The prime whey fed pork legs are cured in a mixture of apple juice, honey, curing salts and local herbs and then lightly smoked over wood chips and air dried for up to a year. The result is truly delicious!

Starter
Serves 4

Preparation Time:
20 mins

Cooking Time:
5 – 10 mins

Oven Temperature:
350°F; 180°C; Gas 4

Ingredients:
- 110g (4 oz) cream cheese
- 110g (4oz) Denhay air dried ham
- 12 asparagus spears cooked and cut in half
- 1 small clove garlic crushed
- salt and freshly ground black pepper

Combine cream cheese, garlic, salt and pepper. Spread slices of ham with the cheese mixture and roll around 2-3 asparagus segments.
Arrange on a baking sheet and bake lightly until heated through, about 5 minutes.

GRILLED CAPRICORN GOATS CHEESE WITH CRISPY BACON SALAD

Fiona James
Westcountry Cooking Project Officer
Taste of the West
Agriculture House,
Pynes Hill, Exeter
01392 440745

Starter
Serves 4

Preparation Time:
20 mins

Cooking Time:
15 mins

Trained at Leith's School of Food & Wine, Fiona worked at a number of renowned London Restaurants.

Mix the salad dressing ingredients in an old jam jar or any screw top jar and shake vigorously until amalgamated. Keep in the fridge until required and give it another jolly good shake before serving.

Place the kernels on a baking sheet and pop under a hot grill for a couple of minutes, shake to turn them so that they brown evenly.

Grill or fry the bacon rashers until crispy. Cool on absorbent kitchen towel to remove some of the grease and when cool snip into pieces.

Cut the goats cheese in half and place under the same hot grill with the skin side down. Cut the toast into rounds about the same size at the goats cheese.

Place the toast in the centre of the plate, carefully scatter the mixed lettuce leaves around the toast. Scatter the bacon bits and pine kernels over the salad around the toast.

The goats cheese should now have started to brown and bubble. Carefully lift off the tray and place on the toast circle. It may be easier to remove the toast circle from the plate and bring it to the cheese and then reintroduce it!

Drizzle a little of the salad dressing over the salad being careful not to overdress the salad as it will be quite salty from the bacon and cheese.

Ingredients:
- 2 x 100g Capricorn Goats cheese
- Bag of fresh mixed salad leaves
- 4 tbsp good salad dressing
- 2 tbsp pine kernels (optional)
- 110g (4oz) smoked streaky bacon rashers
- 4 slices of white bread toasted lightly

Salad Dressing:
- 1 tsp your favourite mustard
- 1 tsp sugar
- salt and freshly ground pepper
- 100ml (4 floz) olive oil
- 50ml (2 floz) Balsamic vinegar
- 1 tsp sesame oil (optional)

ROAST PORK WITH BACON AND SPINACH STUFFING

Main Course
Serves 4

Preparation Time:
30 mins

Cooking Time:
3 hours (depending on weight of joint)

Oven Temperature:
Gas Mark 5; 375°F; 190°C

Ingredients:
- 1.25kg (2 ½ lb) rolled leg or loin joint
- 4 rashers of back bacon chopped
- 1 onion chopped
- 1 clove garlic crushed
- 1 tbsp oil
- 75g (3oz) frozen spinach, thawed
- 110g (4oz) fresh breadcrumbs
- 1 tbsp red pesto
- ½ lemon grated rind and juice
- salt and ground black pepper

Glaze:
- 2 tbsp lemon curd mixed with 1 tbsp lemon juice

Lashbrook Unique Country Pork
Lashbrook Farm, Talaton
Exeter EX5 2RU
01404 850228
email: john@lashbrookpork.co.uk

The fine quality and delicious, unique taste of Lashbrook pork and bacon can be appreciated by simply cooking it in time honoured ways. Lashbrook pork comes from traditional breeds of pig reared free range in the fields near Talaton, Devon. The herd of British Saddleback sows has been at Lashbrook for over 35 years, together with the Large White and Welsh breeds, producing highly contented pigs.

The sustainable cropping system allows the pigs to move round the farm, adding fertility to the fields where the cereal and potato crops are later sown. The pigs use the grain for feed and straw for bedding, as well as clearing up any waste potatoes and rooting the soil for weeds.

Lashbrooks Unique Country Pork and Bacon, plus the award winning sausages, are all available by mail order, and can be viewed through their website www.lashbrookpork.co.uk.

Fry the bacon, onion and garlic in the oil until cooked. Mix with the rest of the stuffing ingredients.

Lay out the pork join and spread the stuffing over it. Roll up and tie with string.

Weigh the pork and cook for 30 mins per 450g (1 lb) plus an extra 30 mins.

Mix the glaze ingredients and brush over the joint 20 minutes before the end of the cooking time and again around 10 minutes before the end.

This recipe was taken from "Pork Perfection" original recipes by Paula Deacon for Lashbrook Unique Country Pork.

DENHAY CHEDDAR AND BACON PUDDING

Denhay Farms Ltd
Broadoak
Bridport
Dorset DT6 5NP
01308 422770
George and Amanda Streatfeild
www.denhay.co.uk

Denhay Farms Ltd produce superb award winning Air Dried Ham and Dry Cured Bacon, together with their Farmhouse Cheddar using the traditional skills and techniques employed in the Marshwood Vale and West Country for generations. Denhay Farm is set in an area of outstanding natural beauty and uses the original West Country cycle; lush grass to feed the dairy herd to make cheese; the whey from the cheese to feed the pigs; the muck from the pigs to fertilise the grass to feed the cows.

Denhay has over 950 Friesian Holstein cows selected for the high protein quality of their milk. All the milk produced on the farm is used to make Traditional Farmhouse Cheddar, cream and butter.

Arrange half the buttered bread in shallow oven proof dish. Lightly fry the bacon and layer on top of the bread with the cheese. Season and add the vegetables.

Cover with the remaining bread triangles. In a bowl whisk the eggs, add the Worcester sauce, mustard and milk. Pour over the bread and leave for an hour in the fridge.

Bake for 25-30 minutes at 190°C; 365°F; Gas Mark 5 until golden brown.

Serve with salad.

Main Course
Lunch or light supper dish
Serves 4

Preparation Time:
30 mins (plus 1 hour standing time)

Cooking Time:
30 mins

Oven Temperature:
190°C; 375°F; Gas 5

Ingredients:
- 10 slices of brown or white bread cut into triangles and buttered
- 225g (8 oz) back or streaky Denhay bacon
- 175g (6 oz) Denhay cheddar grated
- 1 pepper sliced
- 1 onion or leek chopped
- 4 eggs beaten
- 600ml milk
- 1 small tsp mustard
- few drops Worcestershire sauce

PORK, BACON AND SAUSAGES

PORK FILLET WITH APRICOTS AND WEST COUNTRY CIDER

Main Course
Serves 4

Preparation Time:
25 mins

Cooking Time:
30 mins

Ingredients:
- 450g (1lb) pork tenderloin
- 1 onion
- 50g (2oz) butter
- 1 tbsp grain mustard
- 2 tsp flour
- 300ml (½ pint) West Country cider
- 110g (4 oz) ready to eat apricots
- 150 ml (5 floz) double cream

Trengilly Wartha Inn
Nancenoy
Constantine
Falmouth
Cornwall 01326 340332

Winners of Best Pub in the South West Region 2000.

Trengilly Wartha is a traditional inn set in spectacular countryside close to the Helford River. You can enjoy a simple bar snack or more elaborate food in the bar at lunch and dinner. The fine restaurant is open for dinner only. Real ales, a wide range of malt whiskies and over 200 wines add to the enjoyment.

Trim the pork of any fat or sinew and cut into ½ inch thick medallions.

Soak the apricots in the cider so that they absorb the cider flavour.

Dice the onion very finely. Melt the butter in a heavy based saucepan and add the onion. Turn the heat to low and gently fry the onion for 15 minutes until soft but not coloured (to prevent colouring place a scrunched up sheet of wet greaseproof paper over the top of the onion in the pan).

Stir the mustard into the onion mix and cook on medium heat for 1 minute.

Dust the pork medallions in flour.

Turn up the heat and add the pork – cooking until browned.

Season well with salt and pepper.

Add the apricots and cider, bring to the boil stirring occasionally to prevent it from sticking.

Turn down to a simmer. Add the cream and bring to the boil and simmer gently to thicken. Adjust the seasoning with a little lemon juice and salt and pepper.

Serve with warm buttered noodles.

DEVON PORK IN MUSTARD SAUCE

The Old Bakehouse
Chulmleigh
01769 580074

A 16th century Wool Merchant's House now accommodates the Old Bakehouse Restaurant and its four guest rooms. By day an ambitious range of full meals and light bites is served, made with locally sourced, additive free ingredients as well as organic vegetables. In the evenings a more decorous candlelit elegance prevails.

Slice pork on diagonal into half inch thick medallions.

Heat large heavy bottomed frying pan. When very hot put a layer of pork slices in the pan and grind over the pepper. Let the slices brown for 1 –2 mins then turn over, sprinkle with salt and brown the other side for a further 1-2 mins. Remove to a plate and repeat until all the slices are browned.

Put in the onion slices, stock and wine into the pan. Let the liquid bubble whilst deglazing with a wooden spoon to scrape all the sediment off the bottom of the pan. Cover and cook on a high heat for 2 – 3mins.

Add peppers and garlic, stir and cover. Cook for 4 or 5 mins, until onions are cooked but still crisp.

Add the mustards and mix well. Stir in 2 tbsp of crème fraiche and heat through – but do not boil.

Return the pork slices and any meat juices that have accumulated. Sprinkle in the cayenne pepper and cook until the pork is heated through. Do not let the sauce boil as it will split. Add further ½ tbsp crème fraiche and stir well. Sprinkle with parsley and serve.

Serve with rice or creamed potatoes.

Main Course
Serves 4

Preparation Time:
10 mins

Cooking Time:
40 mins

Freezing:
Not suitable

This dish has a very low fat content.

Ingredients:
- 2 well trimmed pork tenderloins (approx 700g / 24 oz total)
- salt and ground pepper to taste
- 2 large Spanish onions cut into wedges
- 120ml / 4 floz stock
- 60 ml / 2 floz white wine
- 3 peppers (mixed colours) cut into half inch strips
- 2 cloves garlic minced
- 2 rounded tsp grain mustard
- 1 rounded tsp Dijon mustard
- 2 ½ tbsp crème fraiche
- pinch of cayenne pepper
- 1 tbsp chopped parsley

PILGRIMS PORK FILLET WITH BACON AND SAGE

The Pilgrim's Rest Restaurant and Bistro

Lovington, Somerset 01963 240597

The Pilgrims Rest is a delightful pub/restaurant situated between Castle Cary and Lydford. Fish and seafood is their first love and speciality, everything is prepared and freshly cooked on the premises using high quality local produce where possible.

This dish is a Pilgrim's Rest original and a guaranteed winner. It is very simple to prepare and cook but the result both looks and tastes as if an enormous amount of effort has gone into it. The recipe incorporates the traditional pork flavourings of sage and onion together with apples from the cider. The bacon helps the dish to look fantastic as well as providing the fat to emulsify the liquid and thicken the sauce, protects the pork and keeps it moist and succulent as well as reinforcing the flavour.

To Prepare:

Lay a rasher of bacon on the board with the flat (rind) side on the left and wide end of medallion nearest you. Lay another rasher with flat side on right and medallion away from you, interlocking with and slightly overlapping the first rasher in places down the centre. This should give a rectangular sheet of bacon with no large holes in it.

Season with pepper.

Lay two or three sage leaves across the width of this sheet an inch or so up from the end nearest you.

Lay a piece of pork fillet on top of the sage, the bacon should be about as wide as the fillet is long.

Pick up the edge of the bacon nearest you and roll the fillet away from you, wrapping it in the bacon firmly. You should now have a neatish sausage of bacon wrapped pork.

Tie twice with kitchen string and repeat for the four parcels.

Refrigerate for anything from 2 to 24 hours as this will make the pork easier to handle.

To Cook:

Preheat the oven.

Peel and finely slice the shallots lengthways.

Over a fairly high heat warm the oil in a oven proof sauté or pan casserole which has a lid. When it is hot add the parcels of pork and turn them so that all sides colour a little.

Add the sliced shallot and almost immediately add the cider.

Bring to the boil and when bubbling take the pan off the heat. Cover and put in the oven for 20 to 25 minutes. The pork should be cooked through, but not over cooked.

Lift the pork parcels out of the liquid and keep them warm. Reduce the shallot and cider liquor. When it becomes syrupy it is ready – check the seasoning.

Remove the strings from the pork and slice into 4 or 5 rounds, overlap in the centre of a plate and pour the sauce over the pork.

Serve with new potatoes and salad, or seasonal vegetables.

Main Course
Serves 4

Preparation Time:
30 mins

Cooking Time:
30 mins

Marinade Time:
2 - 24 hours

Oven Temperature:
200°C; 400°F; Mark 6

Ingredients:

- 4 x 175g (6oz) pork fillet (each piece should be around 10-12 cm / 4-5 inches long, trimmed of any fat or sinew)
- 8 rashers of good smoked back bacon without rinds
- 12 leaves fresh sage
- 1 or 2 long shallots (banana shallots)
- 4 round shallots
- 3 tbsp olive oil
- 600ml (1 pint) medium dry cider
- freshly ground black pepper

FARMERS' MARKET SAUSAGE CASSEROLE

Godford Farm
Awliscombe
Honiton 01404 42825
Sally Lawrence

Winner of Westcountry Cooking's 2001 Best Farmhouse Food. Guests return again and again to this award winning farm to have a "special breakfast". Ingredients are sourced locally and are good and wholesome served in large portions in the beautiful old farmhouse.

There are so many delicious sausages available from Farmers' Markets today. This makes an easy and wholesome supper dish whilst using some fabulous West Country sausages.

Peel and slice carrots, onions and dice potatoes.

Put into casserole dish with sausages, cider, water, herbs and seasoning.

Cook for 1 hour with lid on.

Mix cornflour with water and stir into casserole to thicken juices.

Core apple and slice then place on top of casserole.

Cook for a further 15 mins with the lid off.

Suggested Accompaniments: Seasonal vegetables, mashed potatoes, leek and potato layer cake.

Variations:

Duck and orange sausages: substitute orange slices for apple.

Beef and mustard sausages: use leeks instead of apple.

Lamb and mint sausages: use red wine and mushrooms instead of apple.

Main Course
Serves 4

Preparation Time:
15 mins

Cooking Time:
75 mins

Oven Temperature:
Gas Mark 4; 180°C; 350°F

Freezing:
Suitable.

Ingredients:
- 8 sausages (pork and apple)
- 2 carrots
- 2 potatoes
- 1 onion
- 1 red apple
- 300ml (½ pint) cider
- 300ml (½ pint) water
- 1 tbsp cornflour mixed with 3 tbsp water
- 1 dsp mixed herbs – fresh or dried
- salt and pepper to taste

Chicken & Duck

DARTS FARM SPICY CHICKEN SALAD

Darts Farm Shopping Village and Café
Topsham
Exeter, Devon
01392 875587

Darts Farm has its own home grown and organic produce together with delicatessen, bakery, Gerald David Butchers and Café. The ultimate 'Farm Shop' experience.

This recipe is really quick and very tasty. It really couldn't be easier. Ottervale Chutney is available at Darts Farm and all good Delicatessens – and is produced in Budleigh Salterton. Ottervale produce a complete range of chutneys and jellies, all made to the highest standards. No artificial colourings or preservatives are used in the production.

Heat a little olive oil in a heavy based frying pan and gently fry off the onion, peppers, garam masala, tumeric and ginger until fragrant and softened.

Increase the heat and add the chicken to the pan, stir frying rapidly until the chicken is cooked through and tender.

Reduce the heat add the chutney and continue to fry for 4-6 minutes until the chicken is cooked through and the sauce is reduced.

Season to taste and add Tabasco as required.

Serve on a bed of mixed salad leaves and top with thinly sliced crispy bacon if desired.

Main Course
Serves 4

Preparation Time:
20 mins

Cooking Time:
15 mins

Ingredients:
- 6 chicken breasts cut into chunks
- 1 tbsp olive oil
- 1 small onion – finely diced
- ½ of each – yellow green and red pepper thinly sliced
- 1 tsp garam masala
- 1 tsp tumeric
- 4 tbsp Ottervale Devon Fire Chutney
- 1 tsp fresh ginger finely chopped (optional)
- salt and pepper to taste
- a few drops of Tabasco (to taste)

Garnish:
4 slices of streaky bacon, fried or grilled until crispy

CHICKEN PARCELS WITH DEVON BLUE SAUCE

Fiona James

Westcountry Cooking Project Officer

Formally trained at Leiths School of Food and Wine and worked in a number of top London Restaurants during the late 1980s. Fiona continued to work in Directors Dining Rooms during the 1990s and cooking for a wide variety of people from Politicians, Douglas Hurd, to actors such as Edward Fox.

To make the parcels:

Slice the Devon Blue into four thin slices.

Fold each chicken breast in half and put a slice of Devon Blue inside the fold of each.

Melt the butter – (15-20 seconds in microwave).

Filo Pastry: Completely unroll the pastry from the packet and with a large knife cut in half by the long side to create two equally sized squares.

Take a clean tea towel and run under the tap and wring out so it is damp. Cover the filo pastry with damp cloth to stop drying out. Dry filo pastry is impossible to handle.

Take a clean, new 1 inch paint brush (or a pastry brush) and butter one square of pastry. Butter a second and place at right angles to the first on top. Butter a third and place at a different angle.

Paint a ring of butter around the edges and place the chicken breast in the middle. Bring all the edges together to form a money bag.

Place the parcels on a baking sheet and bake in the oven for 25 – 35mins depending on the size of the chicken breasts.

To make the sauce:

Finely chop the Spring onions.

Sweat the spring onions in a pan with the butter. When sizzling wet the greaseproof paper and place over the onions and turn the heat down to low. This will cut out all the air and stop the onions from browning. When the onions are glossy, soft and sweet they are done. This should take 5-10 mins.

Add the wine to the pan and bring to the boil. Add the single cream and turn the heat down to medium.

Crumble in the Devon Blue in small pieces and stir until melted through the sauce. Do not boil the sauce at this stage with the cheese incorporated.

You can make this in advance and warm it up later. The skin that forms will soon dissolve back into the sauce.

Always warm the sauce through gently and slowly!

If the sauce is too thick add a dash more wine.

To serve: flood the plate with a spoonful of sauce and place the parcel on the top.

Serve with new potatoes and beans, mangetout, green salad.

Main Course
Serves 4

Preparation Time:
30 mins

Cooking Time:
35 mins

Oven Temperature:
Gas Mark 5; 375°F; 190°C

Freezing:
Suitable to freeze the parcels before cooking

Ingredients:
For the parcels
- 4 chicken breasts or 1 per person
- 1 pack filo pastry
- 110g (4oz) butter – melted
- 50g (2oz) piece Devon Blue cheese

For the sauce
- 1 bunch spring onions
- 200g (7oz) piece Devon Blue cheese
- 50g (2oz) butter
- 150ml (5floz) dry white wine
- 300ml (½ pint) single cream

SIMPLE CREAMY CHICKEN PIE

Janet Gibbs

Janet is a member of the Westcountry Cooking Supporters Club; describes herself as a "serial housewife" and as well as helping co-ordinate Tedburn St Mary's winning entry in the 2001 Village of the Year competition, has a love of cooking and experimenting with simple and traditional foods, as well as the more exotic!

Melt the butter in a saucepan; stir in the flour and cook over a low heat for 2 mins stirring. Gradually add the chicken stock and milk stirring continuously with a wooden spoon.

Bring to the boil. Remove from the heat, add the cream and season to taste.

Chop the cooked chicken into bite size pieces and stir into the sauce, together with the peas. Transfer to the pie dish.

Moisten the edge of the dish, cut off a strip of pastry and place on the edge. Moisten the strip and cover with the pastry top. Seal the two edges by pressing firmly with your thumb. With a knife make small marks around the edges. Make a slit in the top and brush with beaten egg.

Bake in the oven for 30 mins until golden brown.

Serve with new potatoes and seasonal vegetables.

Main Course
Serves 4

Preparation Time:
15 mins

Cooking Time:
30 mins

Oven Temperature:
Gas Mark 6; 400°F; 200°C

Freezing:
Suitable if uncooked

Ingredients:
- 50g (2oz) butter
- 50g (2oz) plain flour
- 150ml (5floz) chicken stock
- 300ml (10floz) pint milk
- 4 tbsp double cream
- salt and pepper
- 350-450g (12 –16 oz) cooked chicken
- 110g (4 oz) frozen peas
- 225g (8 oz) puff pastry
- 1 medium egg

You will also need 1 ½ pint pie dish

BLACK PEPPER AND LEMON CHICKEN

Main Course
Serves 4

Preparation Time:
15 mins

Cooking Time:
30 – 35 mins

Marinade Time:
2 hours

Oven Temperature:
Gas mark 4; 350°F; 180°C

Ingredients:
- 4 large chicken thighs
- 1 large lemon
- 2-3 tbsp olive oil
- 2 tsp golden caster sugar
- 1 tsp black peppercorns
- salt and pepper

June Griffiths
Supporters Club Member

Mix 2 - 3 tbsp olive oil, 2 tsp sugar, the zest and juice of the lemon and black pepper (freshly ground in a pestle and mortar).

Marinade the chicken thighs in this mixture for around 2 hours (or as long as possible).

Place the chicken in a roasting tin and cook in the oven for 30 mins. Baste 2 or 3 times during the cooking time with the juices.

Serve with new potatoes and seasonal vegetables such as mangetout and carrots. Alternatively serve cold with chips and mixed salad.

ROAST DUCK BREASTS WITH RASPBERRIES AND BALSAMIC VINEGAR

Charlton Orchards
Charlton Road, Creech St Michael, Taunton TQ3 5PF
01823 412959

Robin Small / Matthew Freudenberg

Over 30 apple varieties, pears, plums, strawberries, gooseberries and other soft fruit are grown on the farm. Range of apple juices are produced and sold at farmers' markets together with preserves.

The strong flavour of autumn raspberries goes especially well with duck. Their slight acidity balances the richness of the meat.

Main Course
Serves 4

Cooking Time:
30 mins

Preparation Time:
15 mins

Oven Temperature:
220°C; 425°F; Gas Mark 7

Ingredients:
- 450 g (1 lb) autumn or other raspberries
- 2 pieces of star anise
- 4 duck breasts
- sea salt
- 2 tbsp Balsamic vinegar
- freshly ground black pepper

Spread the raspberries over the base of a shallow roasting tin. Bury the star anise amongst the fruit.

Prick the duck breasts thoroughly with a fork, rub the skin with plenty of salt and then place on top of the fruit.

Roast in a preheated oven at 220 C (425 F or Gas Mark 7) for about 30 minutes, or until the duck is cooked as required. Cover for the first 15 minutes.

Allow the duck breasts to stand for 5 minutes before slicing. Meanwhile, remove the star anise and add the Balsamic vinegar.

Puree the fruit with the duck juices in a blender until smooth. Rub the sauce through a sieve to remove the pips and season to taste.

If you require a slightly sweeter sauce, add a little redcurrant jelly.

Slice the duck breasts and serve on a pool of sauce.

DUCK BREAST WITH ORANGE AND COINTREAU SAUCE

Jacqueline's Restaurant & TeaRooms
High Street
Warminster
Wilts 01985 217373

Overall winner of Best Café in the South West Region 2001. Jacqueline's offers high quality home made food served in a relaxed atmosphere with old fashioned courtesy. Wherever possible local produce is featured on the menu and frequently altered to take full advantage of the seasonal wealth of West Country ingredients.

Main Course
Serves 4

Preparation Time:
10 mins

Cooking Time:
9 - 15 mins

Oven Temperature:
Gas mark 7; 220°C; 425°F

Wash and pat dry the duck breasts then score the skin into diamond shapes. Sprinkle the skin fairly liberally with salt and sparsely with freshly ground black pepper. Gently heat a heavy frying pan using no fat or oil and cook the breasts skin side down until golden. Turn over and sear the meat side.

Place skin side up on a trivet and roast in the top of the pre-heated oven – 9 minutes for rare, 12 mins for medium and 14 minutes for well done. Remove from the oven and allow to rest for 5 – 7 minutes before carving.

Whilst the duck is cooking drain the fat from the pan and pour in the orange juice, add the sugar, cloves, zest and season lightly with salt and pepper. Reduce until the juice is translucent and has a syrupy consistency. Add the Cointreau and bring back to the same consistency. Adjust the seasoning to taste.

To serve – carve the duck into five or six slices and place on a hot plate, pour over the sauce.

Serve with new potatoes boiled in their skins and fine beans.

Photo: David Wiltshire of David Wiltshire Photography

Ingredients:
- 4 x 225 (8oz) duck breasts
- 500ml (¾ pint) orange juice
- 50g (2oz) sugar
- 2-3 whole cloves
- zest of one orange
- 100ml (4 floz) Cointreau
- salt and freshly ground black pepper

DUCK BREAST WITH VICTORIA PLUM SAUCE AND CHIVE ROSTI

Main Course
Serves 4

Preparation Time:
15 mins

Cooking Time:
25 mins

Oven Temperature:
Gas Mark 4; 180°C; 350°F

The Edgemoor Hotel
Bovey Tracey
Devon
01626 832466
Rod & Pat Day

The Edgemoor Hotel won the Westcountry Cooking Awards Best Hotel in Devon and were runners up in the overall Hotel category across the six counties. The Edgemoor is a delightful Country House standing in 2 acres of grounds in a peaceful wooded setting in the boundary of the Dartmoor National Park. The monthly changing menu often incorporates many West Country specialities as does the Bar Menu and Specials Board.

Ingredients:

- 4 duck breasts – each weighing (8 –10oz) 225 - 300g
- 6 – 8 victoria plums
- 75 ml (3floz) port
- 150 (5 floz) vegetable stock
- 2 large potatoes
- 1 heaped tbsp chopped chives
- salt and pepper to taste

Simmer the plums in vegetable stock and port until soft, liquidise and sieve.

Make rostis by grating the potatoes coarsely, adding chopped chives mix and season well. Form into patty shapes and fry gently until cooked through and golden brown (approx 15 mins).

Score the skin of each duck breast and pan fry for 8 –10 mins then put into a medium oven to finish cooking and crisp the skin (about 8 mins). Put the duck juices (but not the fat) into the plum sauce, season well and reheat gently.

To serve: place the rosti in the centre of the plate, arrange the sliced duck breast over it and surround with sauce. Garnish with slices of orange and julienne of leek.

ROAST DUCK WITH PLUM AND MUSTARD SAUCE

Heaven Scent Herbs
Unit 9
Gidleys Meadow
Christow
Exeter EX6 7QB

01647 252847
Anne Tarrant

A range of hand made mustards, oils, vinegars, jams, jellies, chutneys and conserves using the best ingredients, no artificial preservatives or colourings. Own label mustards and chutneys are available.

Exeter Farmers' Market: Fore Street
2nd Wednesday each month

Preheat oven to 200°C (400°F or Gas Mark 6).

Mix the ingredients for the paste well.

Prick the duck all over with a fork and rub the paste in well. Cover with foil and roast for 45 minutes for duckling or 25 minutes for wild ducks. Crisp the skin by removing the foil 10 minutes from the end.

Remove ducks from the oven and keep warm.

Separate the fat from the juices in the pan and reserve for roasting potatoes.

To the juices add the stock, wine, tomato juice, plums and mustard.

Simmer for 10 minutes. Strain and reduce by boiling. Season to taste.

Main Course
Serves 4

Preparation Time:
20 mins

Cooking Time:
1 hour

Oven Temperature:
Gas Mark 6; 400°F; 200°C

Ingredients:
- 1 duckling or 2 wild ducks

Marinade:
- 25g (1oz) butter
- grated orange zest of 1 orange
- 1 tbsp Heaven Scent Herbs mustard

For the sauce:
- 300 ml (½ pint) stock
- 150 ml (¼ pint) dry white wine
- 150 ml (¼ pint) tomato juice
- 3 ripe plums, stoned
- 1 tsp Heaven Scent Herbs mustard
- pepper to taste

Game & Venison

RED RUBY BEEF AND GAME CASSEROLE

Main Course
Serves 8

Preparation Time:
30 mins

Cooking Time:
2 – 2 ½ hours

Oven Temperature:
Gas Mark 3-4; 160 - 180°C; 300-350°F

Freezing:
Suitable

Ingredients:
- 450g (1lb) Devon Red Ruby rump steak
- 450g (1 lb) venison
- 450g (1 lb) cubed pheasant breast
- 450g (1 lb) thick pork sausages
- 1 large onion
- 110g (4 oz) sliced carrots
- 225g (8 oz) mushrooms
- 1 tsp ground cumin
- 1 tsp allspice
- 3 tbsp tomato puree
- 3 tbsp cranberry sauce or redcurrant jelly
- 600ml (1 pint) beef stock
- ½ bottle red wine
- salt and pepper to taste
- good handful of any of the following; parsley, sage, thyme, bay leaf
- 80g (3 oz) butter for browning meat

Albert Beer

Westcountry Cooking Committee Member. Former Secretary of Devon Cattle Breeders Society. Journalist for North Devon Journal & part-time Exmoor Farmer.

A good wholesome West Country casserole, perfect for sharing with friends and family on a cold winter's evening.

Brown the meat and sweat the onion in the butter in small batches, and transfer to a heavy bottomed casserole with lid.

Add the carrots, mushrooms, spices, herbs, wine and stock, jelly, tomato puree and sausages.

Cook for 2 to 2 ½ hours, stirring occasionally until the meats are tender, in a medium oven.

Serve with: Potato and celeriac mash, kale or curly greens.

VENISON MINUTE STEAKS IN MUSHROOM SAUCE

Anthony Rusher
Anthony is an Exmoor farmer and "enthusiastic amateur foodie" and has been a member of the Westcountry Cooking Committee for the past three years.

Slice the venison into ½ inch steaks, season thoroughly and marinade in olive oil.

Prepare mushrooms and soften in a little butter.

Fry steaks in a small amount of butter and oil. Turn after 2 mins.

Remove to a hot dish and allow to rest. Add the Madeira to the pan and allow to bubble.

Add the cream and mushrooms to the pan pour over the steaks and serve.

Serve with: New potatoes and salad.

Main Course
Serves 4

Preparation Time:
20 mins

Cooking Time:
10 mins

Ingredients:
- 1 loin of venison (approx 700g or 24 oz)
- 225g (8 oz) sliced mushrooms (for special occasions use wild mushrooms)
- small glass of Madeira
- 150ml (5 floz) double cream
- 1 tbsp olive oil
- 25g (1 oz) butter
- salt and pepper

VENISON LIVER WITH A WILD MUSHROOM, SMOKED BACON & JUNIPER BERRY SAUCE

Main Course
Serves 4

Preparation Time:
30 mins

Cooking Time:
25 mins

Oven Temperature:
Cook on the hob

Ingredients:
- 450g (1lb) venison liver – skinned and thinly sliced
- 2 tbsp plain flour
- 250 ml (8 floz) beef stock
- 2 tsp tomato paste
- salt and pepper
- 250 ml (8 floz) red wine
- 2 tbsp raspberry vinegar
- 12 juniper berries – crushed
- 50g (2oz) butter
- 2 tbsp olive oil
- 2 tbsp Worcestershire sauce
- 4 tbsp chopped parsley
- 225g (8 oz) wild mushrooms washed and drained
- 4 slices smoked bacon diced

The Kings Arms
Didmarton, Gloucestershire
Winner of Westcountry Cooking's prestigious Best Pub in the Region Award 2001 and Best Pub in Gloucestershire 2001.

The King's Arms, a 17th century coaching inn, was originally leased from the Beaufort family in 1760 for 1000 years at a rent of six pence per year. The inn, lovingly restored by Nigel and Jane Worrall, now offers a warm and friendly welcome. The renowned 40 seater restaurant offers an excellent and innovative menu using the best fresh locally purchased ingredients.

The Kings Arms, on the edge of the Badmington Estate, is ideally located for exploring the Cotswolds and within a short drive of Bristol and Gloucester, Bath, Cheltenham and Cirencester.

Heat half the butter and olive oil in a pan and cook the bacon until crispy, add the wild mushrooms and crushed juniper berries – cook for a further 2 mins and set aside.

Dry the liver in kitchen towel gently and toss in seasoned flour.

Heat the remaining butter and oil and pan fry the livers for a few minutes then set aside.

Add the red wine to the pan and reduce to half, add the beef stock, tomato paste, Worcestershire sauce, raspberry vinegar and reduce again. Finally add 1 tbsp of sieved flour and whisk gently until the sauce begins to thicken.

Add the liver, smoked bacon and wild mushrooms to the sauce and cook for a further 2 to 4 minutes depending upon how pink you like the liver.

Garnish with chopped parsley (preferably flat parsley) and serve with onion and parsley mash.

Onion and Parsley Mash:
Peel, chop and boil potatoes until soft, drain and mash with butter milk and seasoning. Add a small diced onion sauted and 2 tbsp chopped parsley.

ROAST LOIN OF VENISON WITH BLACK PUDDING AND A BLACK TREACLE SAUCE

The Pencubitt Hotel
Lamellion Cross, Liskeard, Cornwall 01579 342694
2001 Winner of Westcountry Cooking Awards:
Best Hotel in Cornwall
Best Hotel in South West

Quality independent hotel situated just outside the historic market town of Liskeard. Emphasis is placed on the cuisine at Pencubitt with the very best ingredients being sourced locally to produce the highest quality dishes, absolutely fresh and full of flavour.

Mix the marinade ingredients and marinade the venison for 24 hours.
Remove the venison from the marinade.
Strain the marinade to remove the vegetable brunoise and fry until brown.
Add all the red wine to the vegetables and reduce until a syrupy consistency.
Add the stock and reduce again until a gravy consistency.
Strain the sauce through a fine sieve and discard the vegetables.
Add the treacle to the remaining sauce to taste.
Whisk in the butter and season to taste.

To cook the venison
Sear the venison in a hot pan to brown all sides.
Place in a very hot oven for 8 to 10 minutes and still pink in the middle.
Remove from the oven and leave to rest for 10 minutes.
Slice the venison neatly and season well but leave on a baking sheet.
Place the rested venison back into the oven for a couple of minutes only.

Whilst the venison is cooking:
Cut the black pudding into slices and fry in a little oil until crisp.

To Serve:
Place the black pudding in the centre of a dinner plate, arrange the venison on top and pour a little sauce over the venison.

Suggested Accompanying Vegetables:
Bubble and Squeak (placed under the black pudding).
Caramalised baby onions.

Main Course
Serves 4

Preparation Time:
30 mins

Cooking Time:
1 hour

Oven Temperature:
Gas Mark 8; 450°F; 230°C

Marinade Time:
24 hours

Ingredients:
- 700g (24oz) loin fillet of venison

Marinade:
- olive oil
- 2 bay leaves
- handful of fresh thyme
- rosemary
- 2 cloves garlic
- vegetable brunoise (finely diced carrot, celery, onion)

- 1.2 litres (2 pints) brown stock (preferably game stock)
- 1 bottle red wine
- 2 tsp black treacle
- 25g (1 oz) unsalted butter
- salt and pepper
- 225g (8oz) black pudding
- vegetable oil

ACKNOWLEDGEMENTS

This recipe book would not have been possible without all the hard work and support from around the region by some of our top chefs.

We would like to thank the Meat and Livestock Commission for their kind donation towards to the costs of collating and producing this recipe book.

Our thanks and acknowledgement is offered to the Westcountry Cooking Committee, led by Anthony Gibson, Regional Director of the NFU, Mary James, Albert Beer, Caroline Yates, Anthony Rusher, Michael Raffael, Diane Lethbridge, Sara Paston Williams, William Tullberg, Alan Bartlett and Roger Curnock who not only gave their recipes but offered support and guidance in the production and style of the book.

Thanks also to Jonathan Bosley, photographer, for his hard work and patience during the hectic photoshoot.

Thanks and acknowledgements are also offered to the restaurants, hotels, pubs, chefs and cooks around the region who took the time to write their favourite recipes down and send them in for the book. Without their help this book would not have been possible. These include; Red Snapper Restaurant, Bristol; Nick Coiley at the Agaric in Ashburton; Joyce Molyneux; Paul Da Costa Greaves at The Galley in Topsham; Windrush House, Hazelton; Pencubitt Country House Hotel, Liskeard; Jacqueline's Restaurant and Tea Room, Warminster; Caroline Yates at Confident Cooking; Coombe Estate, Gittisham; Beech Hayes Farm, Taunton; Wild Beef, Chagford; Browns Restaurant, Tavistock; George and Amanda Streatfeild at Denhay Farms Ltd, Bridport; Fiona James, Westcountry Cooking; Lashbrook Unique Country Pork, Talaton; Mike Maguire at Trengilly Wartha, Constantine; The Old Bakehouse, Chulmleigh; The Pilgrim's Rest at Lovington; Sally Lawrence at Godford Farm, Awliscombe; Darts Farm Shopping Village, Topsham; Janet Gibbs; June Griffiths; Charlton Orchards, Taunton; Heaven Scent Herbs, Exeter; The Edgemoor Hotel, Bovey Tracey; Albert Beer, Anthony Rusher and Nigel and Jane Worrall at The Kings Arms at Didmarton.

Recipes were also donated courtesy of Devon Farmers' Market Cook Book. The summer edition of the Devon Farmers' Market Cook Book contains over 100 recipes collected from Farmers' Market stall holders across Devon and can be obtained direct from any Devon Farmers' Market or from Devon Food Links 01392 382213. The Autumn edition will be available from October 2002.

INDEX

Best End of Lamb with Port and Rosemary Sauce	17
Black Pepper and Lemon Chicken	50
Butterflied Leg of Lamb baked in a Salt Paste Crust	18
Charcoal Grilled Brochette of Lamb with Herbs	9
Chicken Parcels with Devon Blue Sauce	47
Christmas Spiced Beef	24
Cornish Beef Carpaccio	23
Cornish Lamb Confit with Caper Sauce	15
Darts Farm Spicy Chicken Salad	45
Denhay Air Dried Ham with Asparagus	31
Denhay Cheddar and Bacon Pudding	35
Devilled Steaks	19
Devon Pork in Mustard Sauce	37
Duck Breast with Orange and Cointreau Sauce	53
Duck Breast with Victoria Plum Sauce and Chive Rosti	54
Farmers' Market Sausage Casserole	41
Grilled Capricorn Goats Cheese with Crispy Bacon Salad	32
Leg of Cotswold Lamb baked in Hay with Herb Butter	13
Loin of Lamb in Filo with Vine Leaves served with a Lemon Mint Sauce	10
Marinated Steaks	21
Noodle Salad with Chilli Beef Cups	25
Pan Fried Fillet of Devon Beef on Roasted Vegetables with Roasted Cherry Tomato Dressing	27
Pan Roasted Breast of Lamb with Saffron, Tomato, and Garlic Bread	11
Pilgrims Pork Fillet with Bacon and Sage	39
Pork Fillet with Apricots and West Country Cider	36
Red Ruby Beef and Game Casserole	58
Roast Chump of Lamb, Shallots, Cherry Tomatoes and Thyme with Wild Garlic mash	7
Roast Duck Breasts with Raspberries and Balsamic Vinegar	51
Roast Duck with Plum and Mustard Sauce	55
Roast Loin of Venison with Black Pudding and a Black Treacle Sauce	61
Roast Pork with Bacon and Spinach Stuffing	33
Simple Creamy Chicken Pie	49
Venison Liver with a Wild Mushroom, Smoked Bacon & Juniper Berry Sauce	60
Venison Minute Steaks in Mushroom Sauce	59

First published in Great Britain in 2002
Copyright© 2002 Taste of the West Ltd

All rights reserved. No part of this publication may be reproduced, stored in a retrieval system, or transmitted in any form or by any means without prior permission of the copyright holder.

British Library Cataloguing-in-publication Data
CIP Record for this title is available from the British Library
ISBN 0-9541074-1-1

Photography: (unless otherwise stated) Jonathan Bosley Photography; Hamlyn House, Mardle Way, Buckfastleigh, Devon TQ11 0NR. Tel: 01364 642910

Designed and Printed by
Acanthus
Blackdown Business Park
Wellington
Somerset TA21 8ST

Tel: 01823 663339
www.acanthuspress.ltd.uk